Piano • Vocal • Guitar

STEVIE NICKS

GREATEST HITS

MW01493945

0117

Cover photo courtesy of Reprise Records, Neal Preston photographer.

ISBN-13: 978-1-4234-3055-1
ISBN-10: 1-4234-3055-7

HAL•LEONARD®
CORPORATION
7777 W. BLUEMOUND RD. P.O. BOX 13819 MILWAUKEE, WI 53213

Visit Hal Leonard Online at
www.halleonard.com

AFTER THE GLITTER FADES

Words and Music by
STEVIE NICKS

BEAUTY AND THE BEAST

Words and Music by
STEVIE NICKS

You're not a stran - ger to me.

My dar-ling lives in a world ____ that is not mine: ____ an old child mis-un-der-stood, out of time.

Time-less is the crea-ture who is wise, ____

BELLA DONNA

Words and Music by
STEVIE NICKS

HAS ANYONE EVER WRITTEN ANYTHING FOR YOU

Words and Music by STEVIE NICKS
and KEITH OLSEN

Has an-y-one ev-er writ-ten an-y-thing

for you   in all your dark-est hours?

EDGE OF SEVENTEEN

Words and Music by
STEVIE NICKS

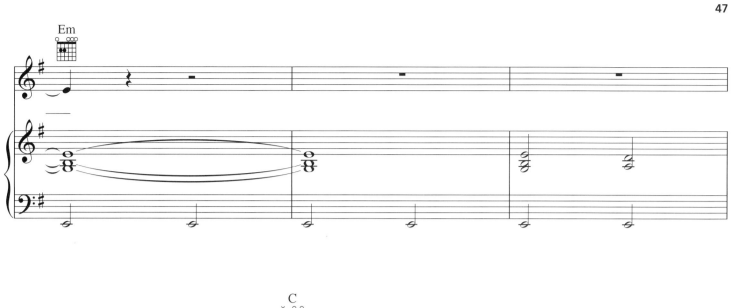

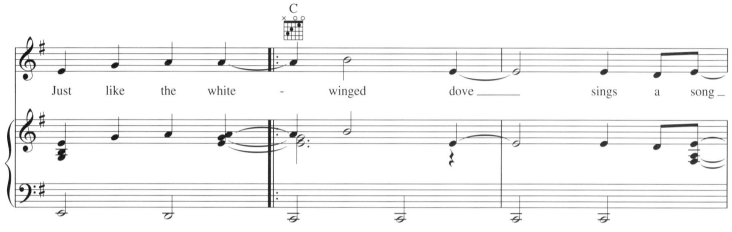

Just like the white - winged dove _____ sings a song _

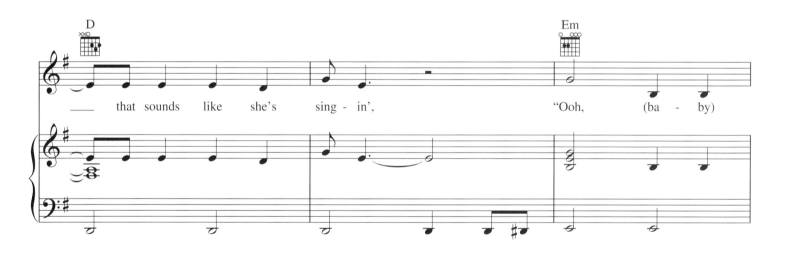

_ that sounds like she's sing - in', "Ooh, (ba - by)

Repeat and Fade

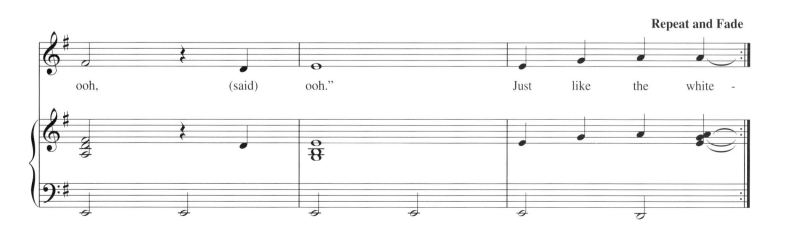

ooh, (said) ooh." Just like the white -

IF ANYONE FALLS

Words and Music by STEVIE NICKS
and SANDY STEWART

I ___ hear a voice ___ in the room ___ next to mine. ___

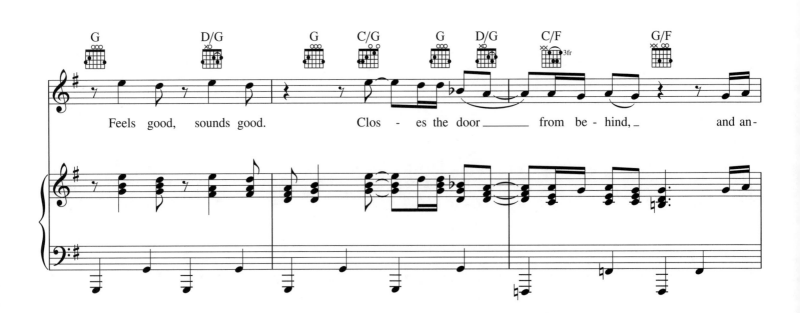

Feels good, sounds good. Clos - es the door ___ from be - hind, ___ and an-

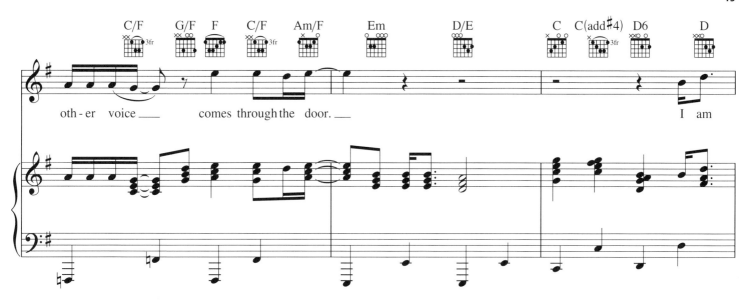

oth - er voice ___ comes through the door. ___ I am

deal - ing ___ with a man. ___ When a - way ___ from me, ___ stays deep in - side ___ my heart.

And he says if an - y - one falls ___ in love, _____ it will be

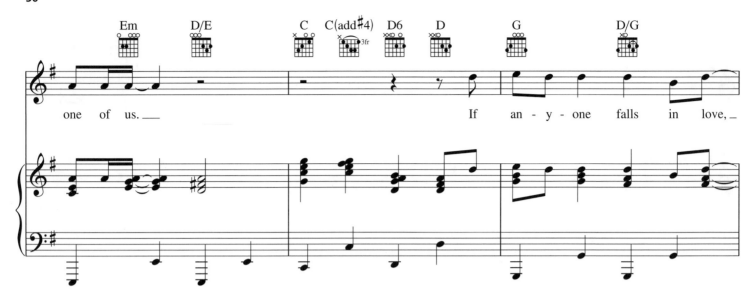

one of us. ___ If an-y-one falls in love, ___

___ some - where ___ in the twi - light, ___ dream - time, ___ some - where ___ in the

To Coda ⊕

back of ___ your mind, _____ if an-y-one falls.

And I heard some - one say _____ as my eyes _____

_____ turned a way, _ he said, _ "I have loved man-y wom-en. I have man-y times

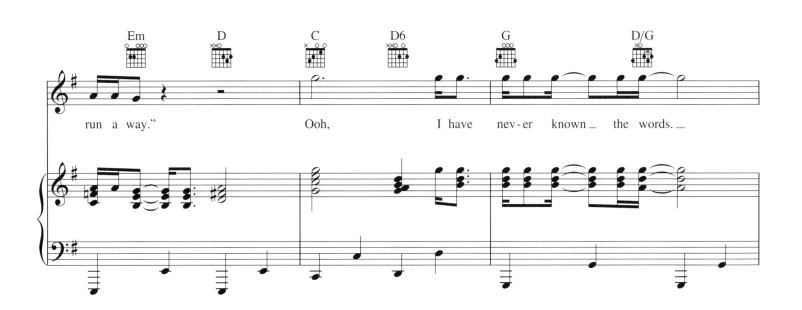

run a way." Ooh, I have nev-er known _ the words. _

Well, I have tried _____ to be

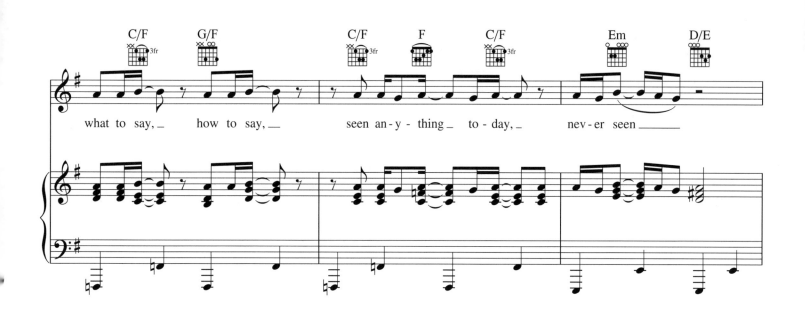

what to say, _ how to say, _ seen an-y-thing_ to-day, _ nev-er seen _____

an-y-thing like you. If an-y one falls in love, ___

some-where _ in the twi-light, _ dream-time, _ some-where _ in the back of __ your mind, ____

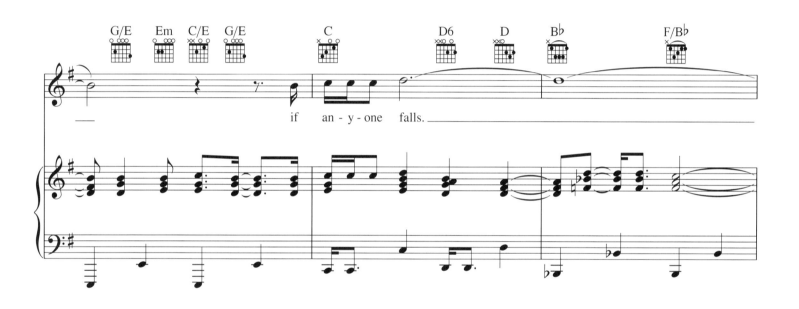

__ if an-y-one falls. _____

__ So I'm nev - er __ gon-na see you (nev - er __ gon-na see you)

deep in - side __ my heart. __ Oh, I see your shad - ow a - gainst, shad - ow a - gainst,

shad - ow a - gainst the wall. __ Ba - by, I see your shad - ow a - gainst the wall. __

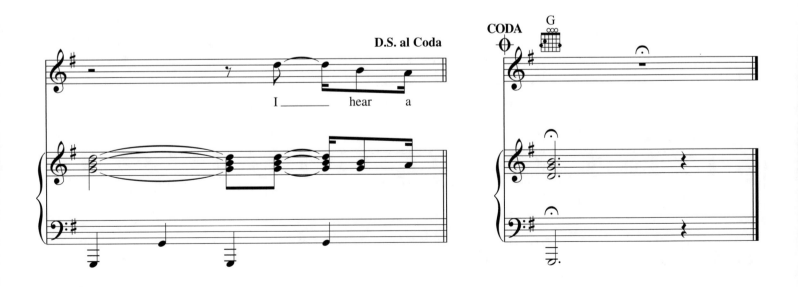

D.S. al Coda

I _____ hear a

CODA

LANDSLIDE

Words and Music by
STEVIE NICKS

Moderately flowing

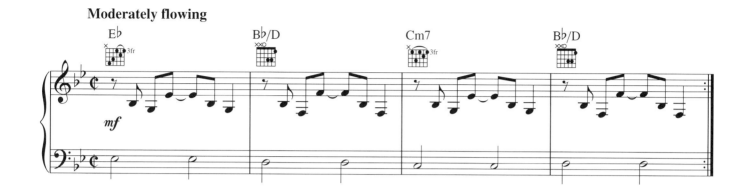

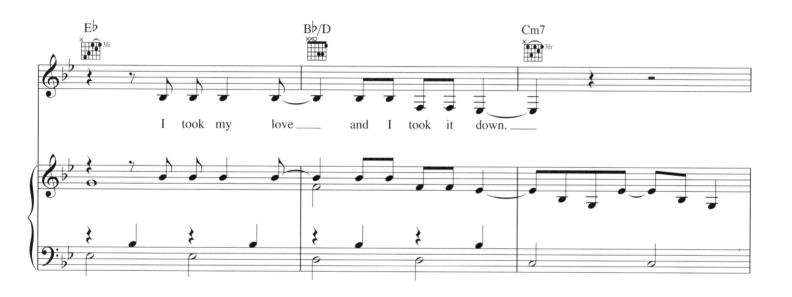

I took my love ___ and I took it down. ___

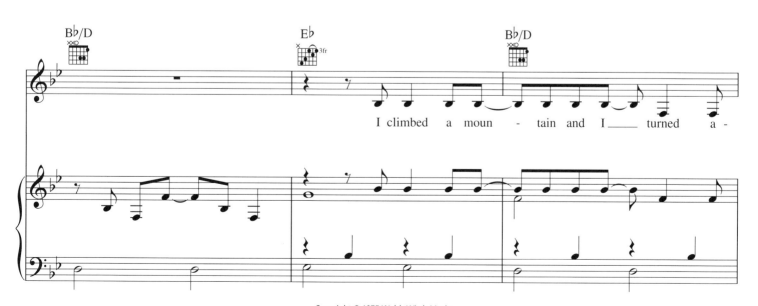

I climbed a moun - tain and I ___ turned a -

LEATHER AND LACE

Words and Music by
STEVIE NICKS

RHIANNON

Words and Music by
STEVIE NICKS

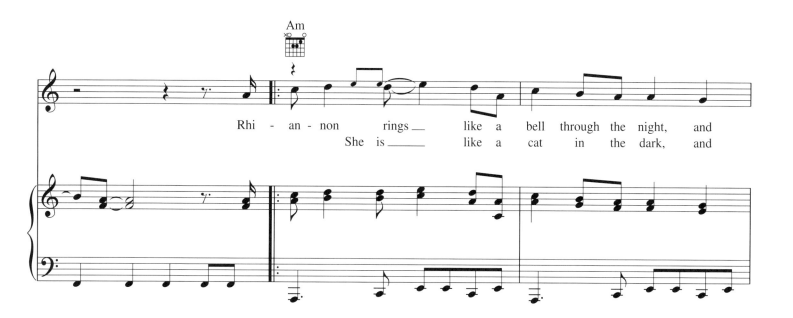

Rhi - an - non rings ____ like a bell through the night, and
She is ____ like a cat in the dark, and

would - n't you love to love ____ her? ____ Takes to the sky like a
then she is the dark - ness. ____ She rules her life like a

bird in flight, ___ and who will be ___ her lov -
fine sky - lark ___ and when the sky ___ is

- er?
star - less.

All your life ___ you've nev - er seen ___ a wom - an ___

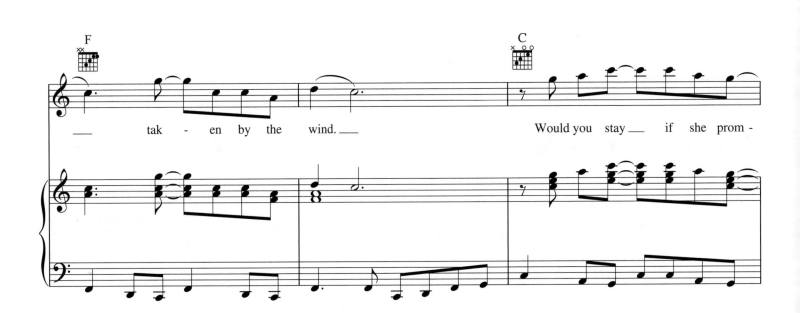

___ tak - en by the wind. ___

Would you stay ___ if she prom -

ROOMS ON FIRE

Words and Music by STEVIE NICKS
and RICK NOWELS

SORCERER

Words and Music by
Stevie Nicks

STOP DRAGGIN' MY HEART AROUND

Words and Music by TOM PETTY
and MIKE CAMPBELL

(Female:) Ba - by,

stop drag - gin' my, stop drag - gin' my heart a - round.

TALK TO ME

Words and Music by
CHAS SANDFORD

I can see we're think-in' 'bout the same things.
Dust - y words ly - ing un - der car - pets
Though we lay face to face and cheek to cheek,

Yes, I see your ex - pres - sion when the phone rings. We both know __ there's
sel - dom heard. Well, must you keep your se - crets locked in - side,
our voic - es stray from the com - mon ground where they could meet. The walls run high, to

some - thing hap - pen - ing here. _____
hid - den deep from view. _____
veil a swell - ing tear. _____

There's no sense in danc in' 'round the sub - ject. A wound gets worse when it's
was is all that hard, is it all that tough? ___ Now, I've shown you all my cards
Let the walls burn down, set your se - crets free. _____ You can break their bonds,

treat - ed with neg - lect. Well, don't turn now there's noth - ing here to
well, is - n't that e - nough? You can hide your hurt but there's some - thin' you can
'cause you're safe with me. You can lose your doubt, 'cause you'll find no dan - ger

STAND BACK

Words and Music by STEVIE NICKS
and PRINCE

Medium Rock beat

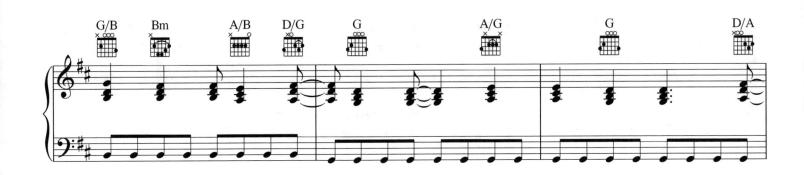

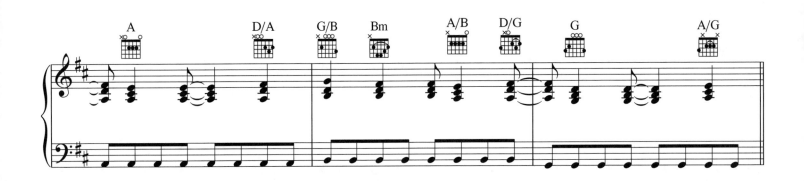

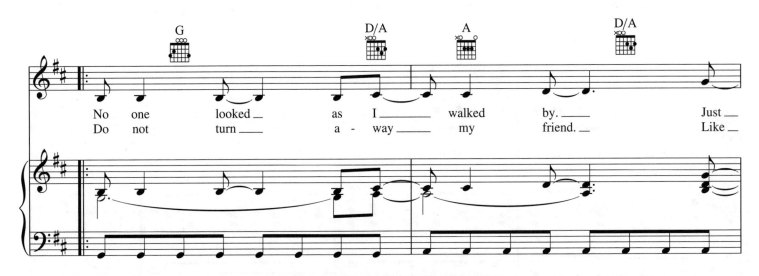

No one looked ___ as I ___ walked by. ___ Just ___
Do not turn ___ a - way ___ my friend. ___ Like ___

stand - ing in a line, ___ (stand - ing in a line, ___) to be

stand - ing in a line. _____ I _____ would

cry. _____ La la la la la ___

___ la la ___ la la ___ la la ___ la